Alfred's Basic Piano Libra

Piano
Musical Concepts Book
Level 4
Theory Worksheets and Solos

This MUSICAL CONCEPTS BOOK reviews and reinforces the most important musical and theoretical concepts introduced in LESSON BOOK 4 of Alfred's Basic Piano Library. Each of the 11 units included consists of a two-page theoretical explanation and worksheet on a specific concept, plus a two-page solo that demonstrates the concept in an attractive musical setting. As all material is new and different from LESSON BOOK 4 and THEORY BOOK 4, the book serves as a valuable and important follow-up in aiding the student to better understand the most important musical concepts being presented.

Instructions for Use

1. MUSICAL CONCEPTS BOOK 4 may be used *after* the student completes LESSON BOOK 4. Used in this way, the book serves as an excellent review of the most important new concepts, while giving the student some additional time before continuing with LESSON BOOK 5.

2. MUSICAL CONCEPTS BOOK 4 may also be used *simultaneously* with LESSON BOOK 4 and THEORY BOOK 4, serving as excellent reinforcement of the most important new concepts at the same time they are being introduced. When used in this manner, assignments are ideally made according to the instructions on the upper right corner of the first page of each unit.

3. Finally, this MUSICAL CONCEPTS BOOK may be used with *any* piano method at a time selected by the teacher. Whichever way this series is used, the student is given an additional opportunity to learn the important and sometimes complex concepts being taught.

Martha Mier • June C. Montgomery

Cover illustration and interior art by Christine Finn

Eighth Note Triplets

The three notes of an EIGHTH NOTE TRIPLET have the same value as two eighth notes or one quarter note.

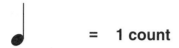 = 1 count

= 1 count

= 1 count

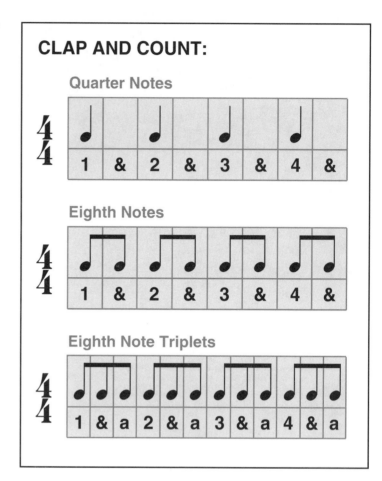

CLAP AND COUNT:

Quarter Notes

| 1 | & | 2 | & | 3 | & | 4 | & |

Eighth Notes

| 1 | & | 2 | & | 3 | & | 4 | & |

Eighth Note Triplets

| 1 | & | a | 2 | & | a | 3 | & | a | 4 | & | a |

For each example below, add the total number of beats that the notes would receive, assuming that the quarter note gets one count. Write the number on the line.

1. [eighth notes] + [triplet] + [half note] = _____

2. [triplet] + [quarter note] + [eighth notes] = _____

3. [whole note] + [dotted half note] + [triplet] = _____

TAP the example on a table top, hands separately, then together, counting aloud each time.

Assuming that the quarter note gets one count, add the number of counts in each rhythm pattern.

Draw a line from each pattern in the left column to the pattern in the right column that has the same number of counts.

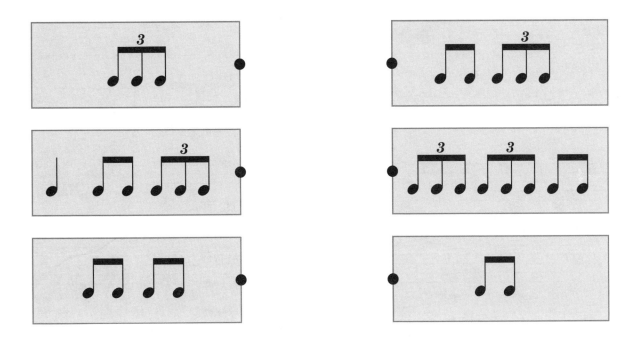

Struttin' in the Sunshine

Moderately, with swing (♫ = ♩ ♪)

Martha Mier

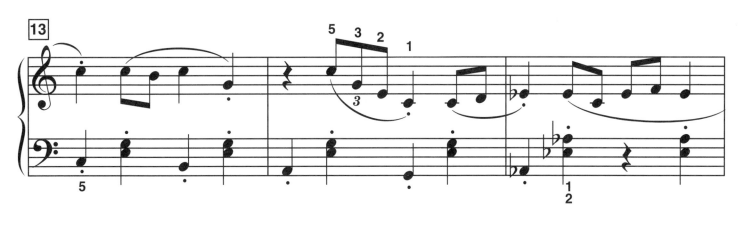

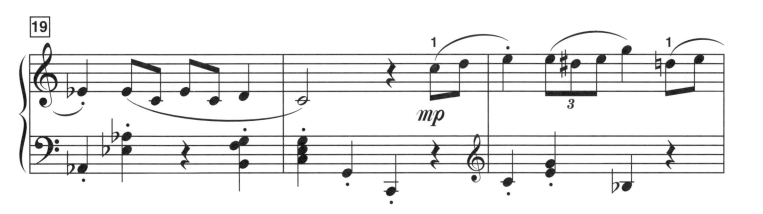

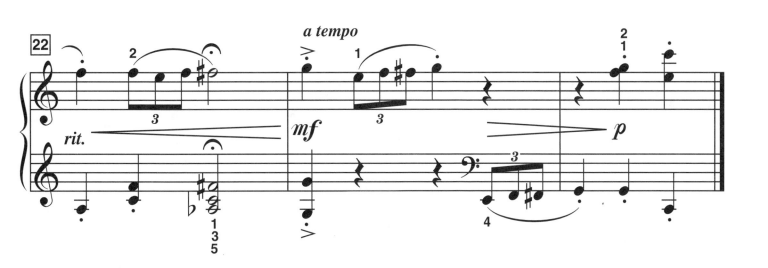

Use after page 7.

Unit 2

Triads: The 1st Inversion

Any ROOT POSITION TRIAD may be inverted by moving the ROOT to the top.

Each triad in the left column is in ROOT POSITION. (The root is the LOWEST note.)

In the right column, do the following:

1. On each keyboard, write letter names showing the same triad in 1st INVERSION. (The root is the TOP note.) Below each keyboard write R (root), 3rd and 5th.

2. On each staff, write the notes of the 1st INVERSION triad, using whole notes. Darken the ROOT of the triad.

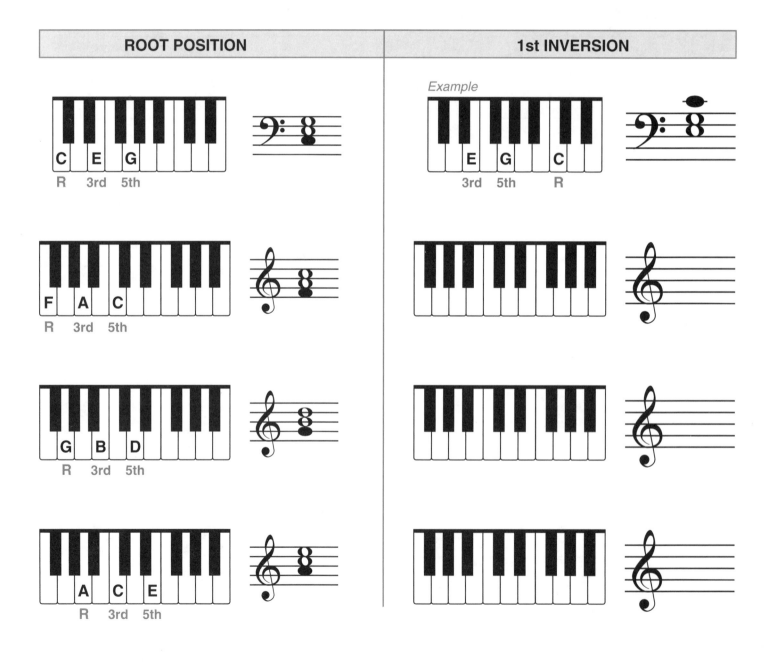

1. On the staff and keyboards below, identify each chord by circling *root position* or *1st inversion*.
2. Circle the ROOT of each triad.
3. On the line, write the chord letter name and its quality (major or minor).

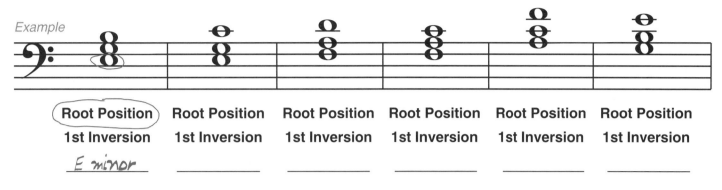

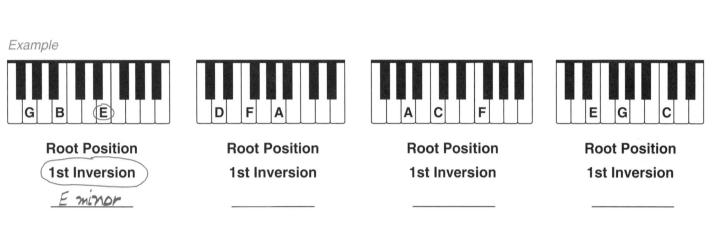

Draw a line from each chord on the staff or keyboard to its matching position
(root position or 1st inversion).

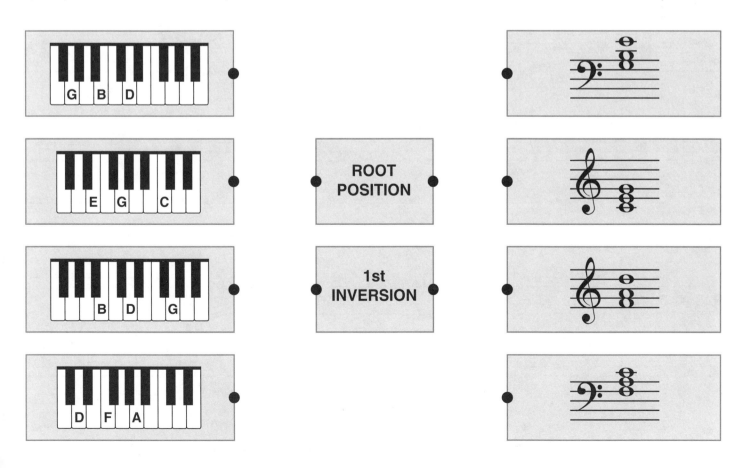

Snow Crystals

Martha Mier

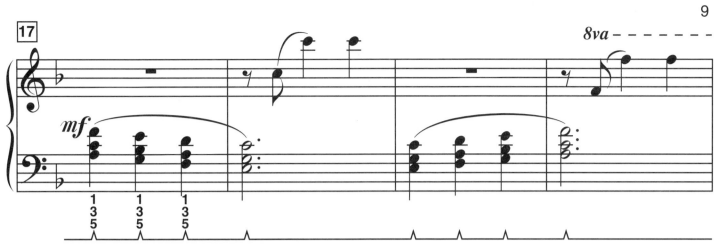

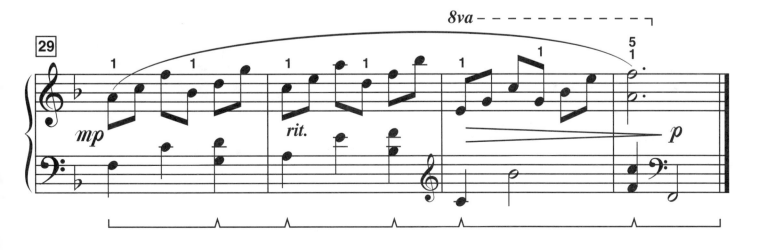

Unit 3

Use after page 13.

Triads: The 2nd Inversion

Any 1st INVERSION TRIAD may be inverted again by moving the lowest note to the top.

Each triad in the left column is in
1st INVERSION. (The root is the TOP note.)

In the right column, do the following:

1. On each keyboard, write letter names
    showing the same triad in 2nd INVERSION.
    (The root is the MIDDLE note.) Below each
    keyboard write R (root), 3rd and 5th.

2. On each staff, write the notes of the 2nd
    INVERSION triad, using whole notes.
    Darken the ROOT of the triad.

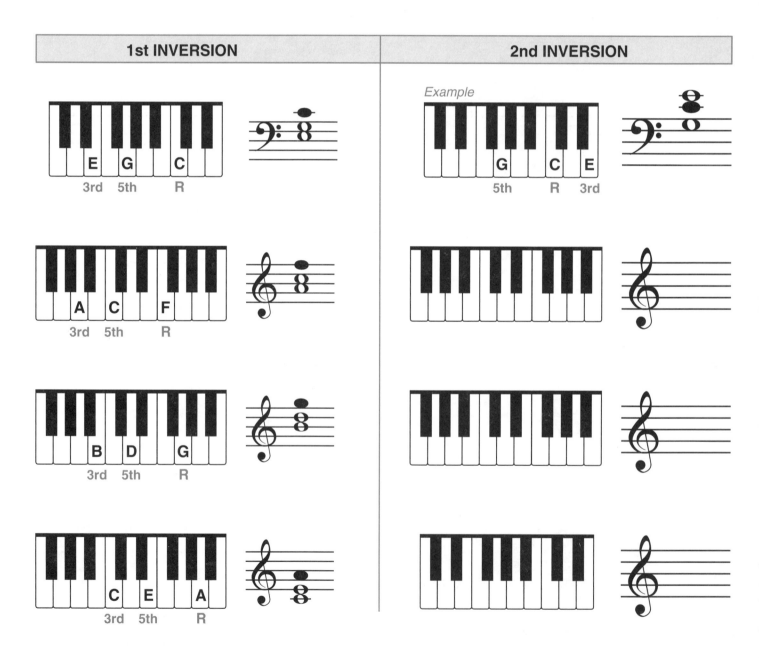

1. On the staff and keyboards below, identify each chord by circling *1st inversion* or *2nd inversion*.
2. Circle the ROOT of each triad.
3. On the line, write the chord letter name and its quality (major or minor).

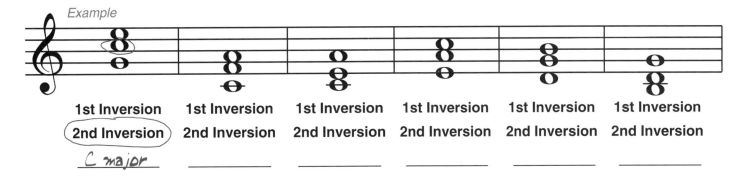

1st Inversion	1st Inversion	1st Inversion	1st Inversion	1st Inversion	1st Inversion
(2nd Inversion)	2nd Inversion	2nd Inversion	2nd Inversion	2nd Inversion	2nd Inversion
C major	_____	_____	_____	_____	_____

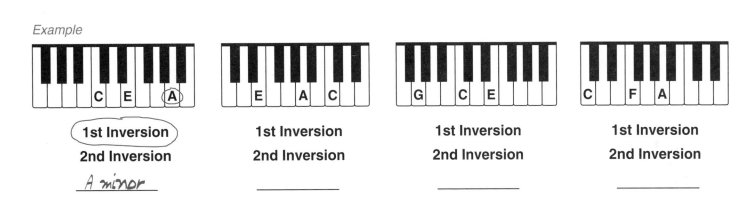

(1st Inversion)	1st Inversion	1st Inversion	1st Inversion
2nd Inversion	2nd Inversion	2nd Inversion	2nd Inversion
A minor	_____	_____	_____

Draw a line from each chord on the staff or keyboard to its matching chord name and inversion.

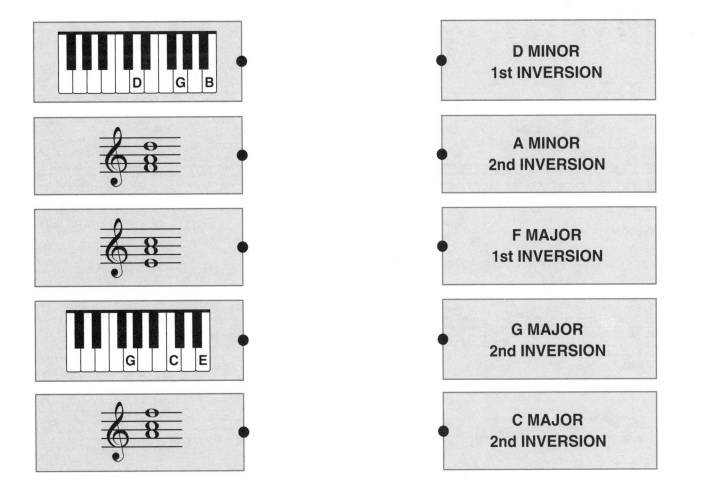

D MINOR 1st INVERSION

A MINOR 2nd INVERSION

F MAJOR 1st INVERSION

G MAJOR 2nd INVERSION

C MAJOR 2nd INVERSION

Olympic Torch

Slowly, with majesty

Martha Mier

Unit 4

Use after page 17.

Triads in All Positions

1. On each keyboard, write letter names to build the indicated triad. Circle the root.

2. On each staff, write the notes of the indicated triad. Darken the root.

	ROOT POSITION	1st INVERSION	2nd INVERSION
C MAJOR	*Example* (keyboard: Ⓒ E G) / staff (treble clef, triad)	(keyboard) / staff (treble clef)	(keyboard) / staff (treble clef)
G MAJOR	(keyboard: G B D) / staff (bass clef)	(keyboard) / staff (bass clef)	(keyboard) / staff (bass clef)
D MAJOR	(keyboard: D F# A) / staff (treble clef)	(keyboard) / staff (treble clef)	(keyboard) / staff (treble clef)

1. Cross out the triads that are *not* in **ROOT POSITION.**

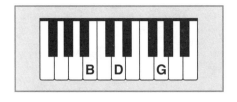

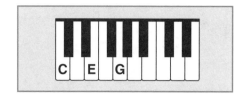

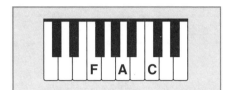

2. Cross out the triads that are *not* in **1st INVERSION.**

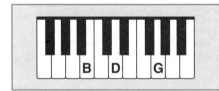

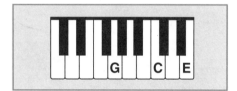

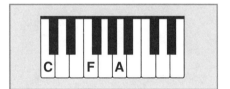
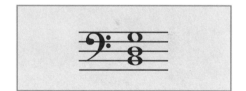

2. Cross out the triads that are *not* in **2nd INVERSION.**

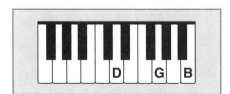

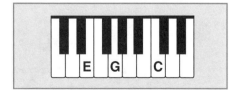

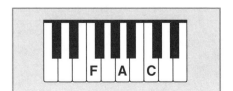

Fiddler Crab Boogie

Martha Mier

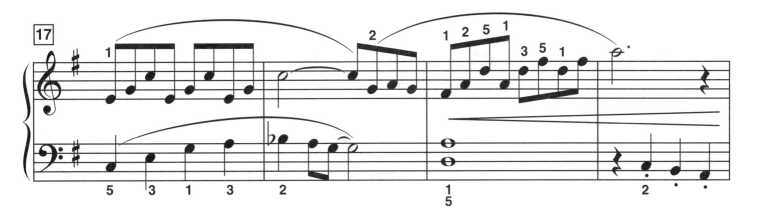

Unit 5

Syncopated Notes

Notes played between the main beats of a measure and held
across the beat are called SYNCOPATED NOTES.

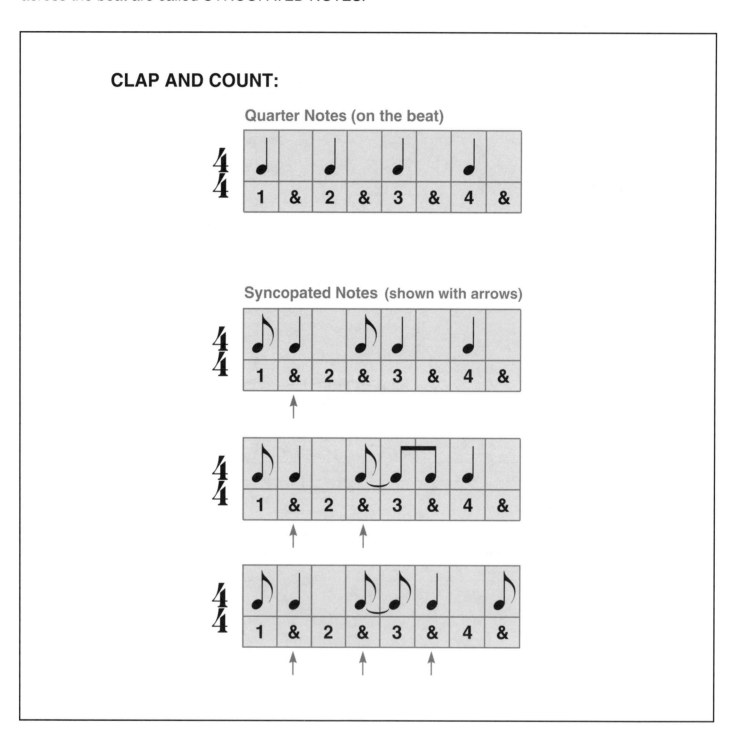

CLAP AND COUNT:

Fill in the blanks:

SYNCOPATED NOTES are played between the _____ _____ of a measure.

They are _____ across the beat.

TAP the examples on a table top, hands separately, then together, counting aloud each time.

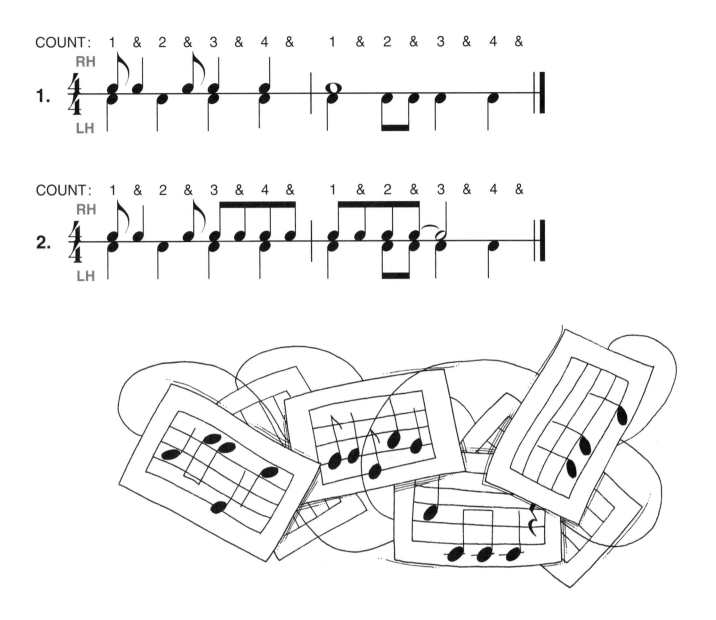

Draw a line from each rhythm to the correct box in the center.

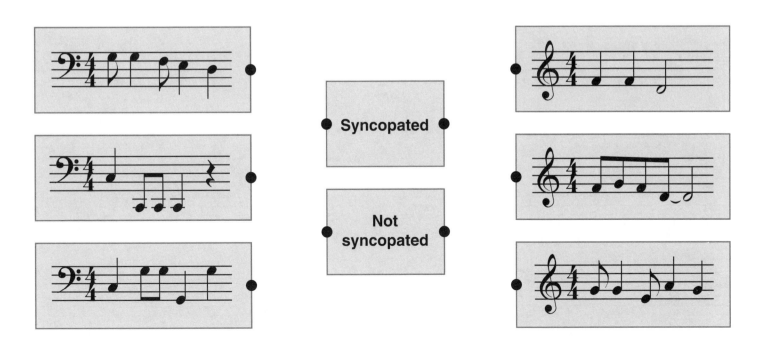

Syncopated

Not syncopated

Mexican Corn Festival

Allegro moderato

Martha Mier

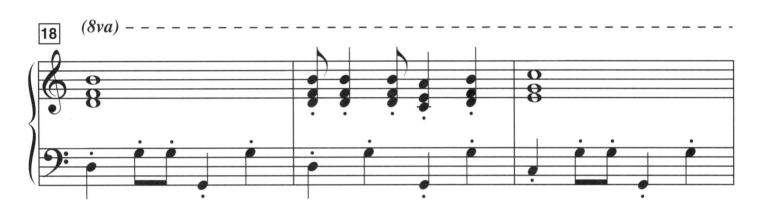

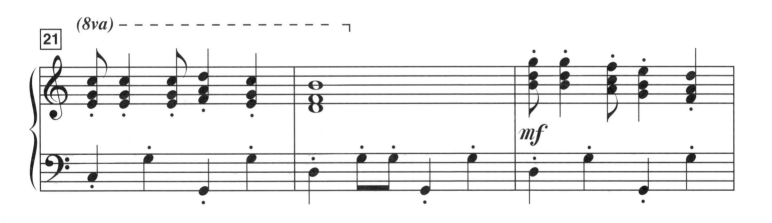

Unit 6

Use after page 25.

Inversions of Seventh Chords

Seventh chords may be inverted in the same way that triads are inverted, by moving the bottom note to the top with each inversion.

On the keyboards, write the notes of the G⁷ chord in ROOT position, 1st inversion, 2nd inversion and 3rd inversion. Circle the root.

ROOT POSITION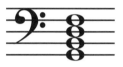

1st INVERSION

2nd INVERSION

3rd INVERSION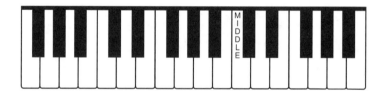

Darken the root of the following seventh chords.

  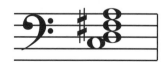

The 5th is often omitted from the seventh chord. This makes it simple to play with one hand.
PLAY with LH.

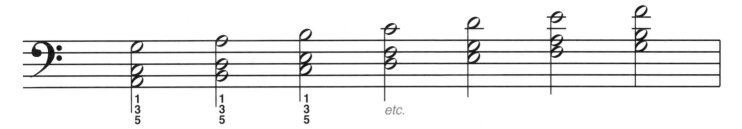

The 3rd is sometimes omitted.
PLAY with LH.

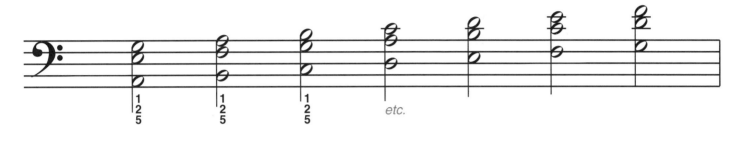

Draw a line from each seventh chord to its matching name.

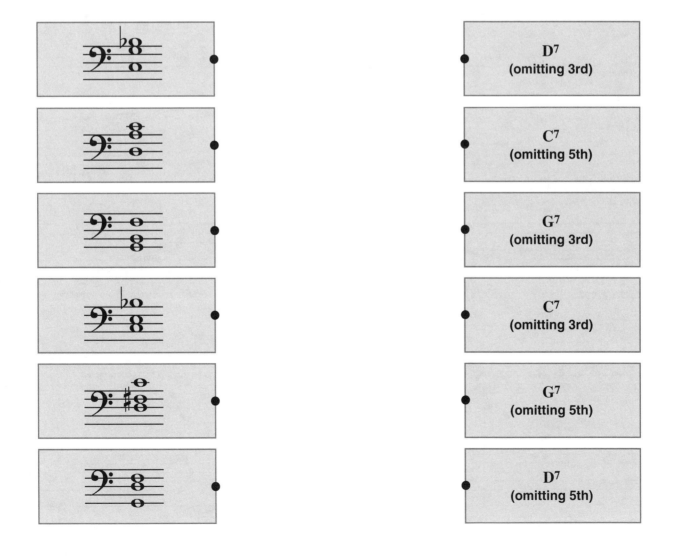

Summer Rainbows

Martha Mier

Slowly, gently

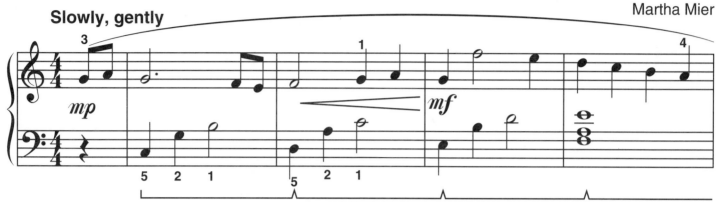

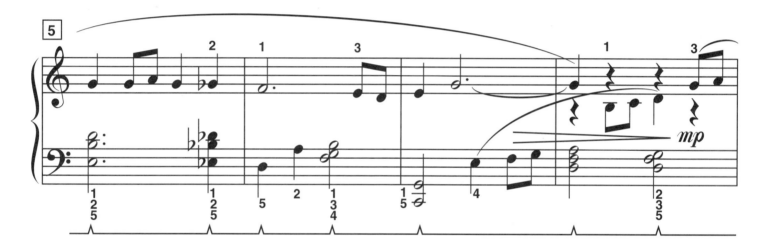

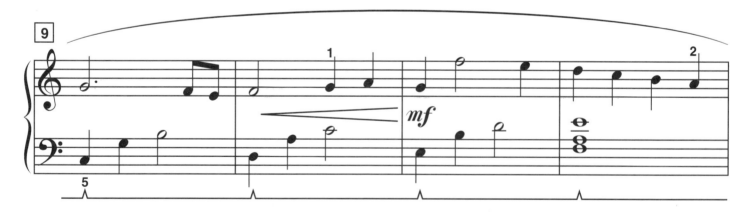

Use after page 29.

Unit 7

The Key of E Minor (Relative of G Major)

Each major key has a RELATIVE MINOR key. It is called "relative" because
it has the same key signature as the major key.

HOW TO FIND THE RELATIVE MINOR SCALE

The relative minor scale begins
on the 6th tone of the major scale.

G MAJOR SCALE

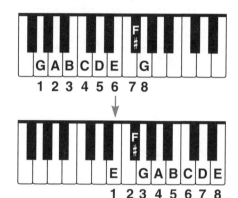

E MINOR SCALE

THE THREE KINDS OF MINOR SCALES

1. NATURAL MINOR SCALE

This scale uses the tones of the relative major scale.

On the keyboard, write the letters of the
E NATURAL MINOR SCALE.

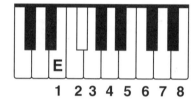

2. HARMONIC MINOR SCALE

The 7th tone (D) is raised one half step,
ascending and descending.

On the keyboard, write the letters of the
E HARMONIC MINOR SCALE.

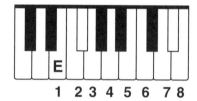

3. MELODIC MINOR SCALE

In the ascending scale, the 6th (C) and 7th (D) tones are raised one half step.
The descending scale is the same as the NATURAL MINOR.

On the keyboards, write the letters of the E MELODIC MINOR SCALE, ascending and descending.

Ascending ———▶   ◀——— **Descending**

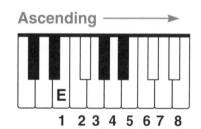   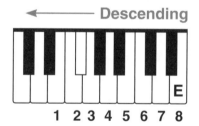

Using the fingering below, play the E natural, harmonic and melodic minor scales hands separately,
then together, ascending and descending.

	Ascending	Descending
RH	1 2 3 1 2 3 4 5	5 4 3 2 1 3 2 1
LH	5 4 3 2 1 3 2 1	1 2 3 1 2 3 4 5

Primary Triads—Key of E Minor

The PRIMARY TRIADS are built on the 1st, 4th and 5th notes of the HARMONIC MINOR scale. Since the triads built on the 1st and 4th notes are minor triads, lower case Roman numerals are used (**i** and **iv**). The triad built on the 5th note is a major triad, so an upper case Roman numeral is used (**V**). A seventh is often added to the **V** chord to create a seventh chord (**V⁷**).

Primary Triads in the Key of E Minor

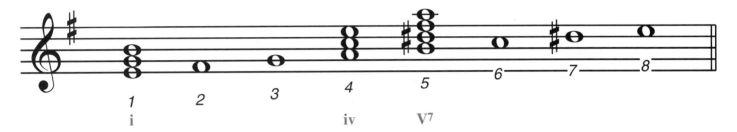

On the keyboards below, write the letter names for the notes of the primary triads in the key of E minor.

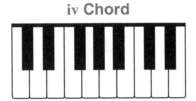
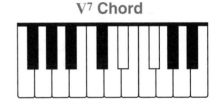

To make playing the **i**, **iv** and **V** (or **V⁷**) chords smoother moving from one to the other, the notes may be rearranged. The same notes must be used, but they may be played in different octaves.

Practice the following E MINOR CHORD PROGRESSION, hands separately, then together. Say the chord names as you play.

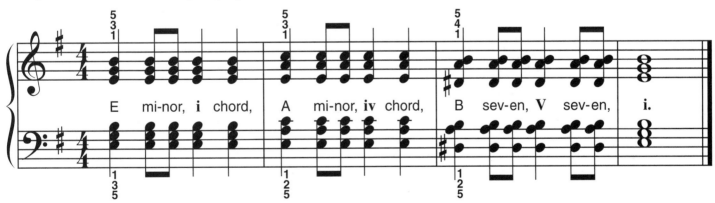

On the top line below the staff, write the Roman numeral name (**i**, **iv** or **V⁷**) of the chord in the key of E minor.
On the bottom line, write the letter name (Em, Am or B⁷) of the chord.

Old English Castle

Martha Mier

Use after page 33.

Unit 8

Sixteenth Notes

Four sixteenth notes have the same value
as two eighth notes or one quarter note.

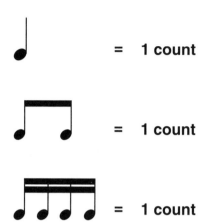

= 1 count

= 1 count

= 1 count

For each example below, add the total number of beats that the notes would receive,
assuming that the quarter note gets one count.

1. _____ + _____ + _____ = _____

2. _____ + _____ + _____ = _____

3. _____ + _____ + _____ = _____

TAP the examples on a table top, hands separately, then together, counting aloud each time.

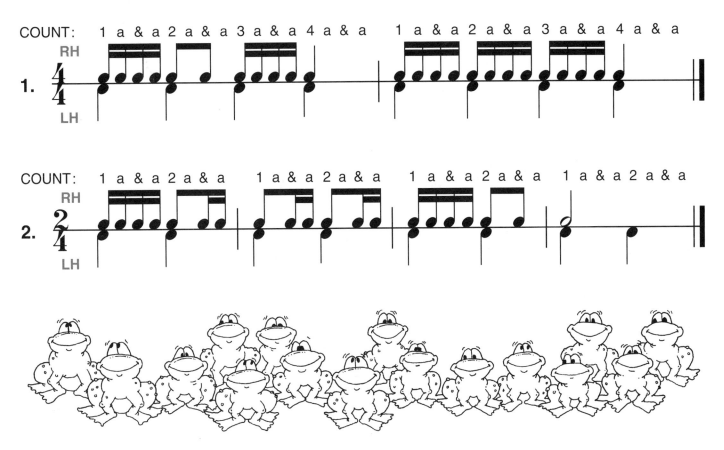

Assuming that the quarter note gets one count, add the number of counts in each rhythm pattern.

Draw a line from each pattern in the left column to the pattern in the right column that has the same number of counts.

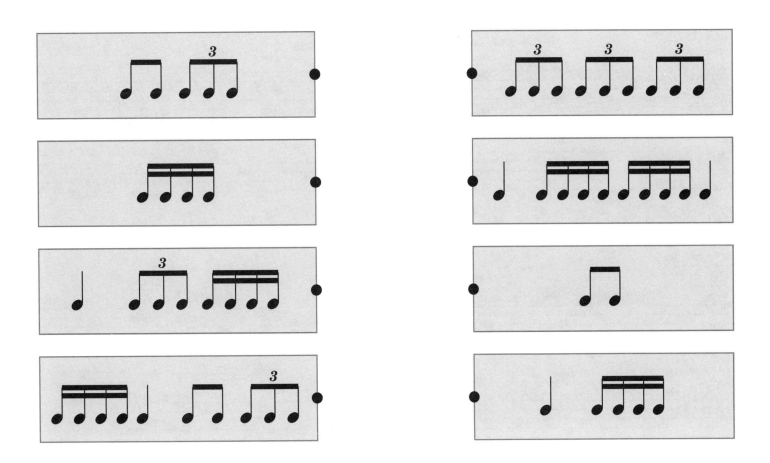

Sonatina in G Major

Martha Mier

Use after page 35.

Unit 9

The Dotted Eighth Note

Dotted rhythms in $\frac{4}{4}$ time each have the same number of pulses (3 pulses for the dotted note and 1 pulse for the short note), although the notes have different values:

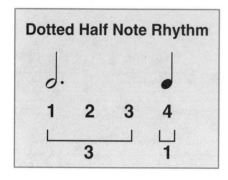

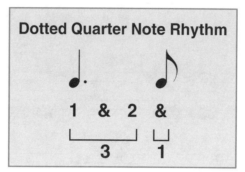

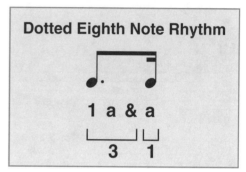

CLAP AND COUNT:

Dotted Half Note Rhythm

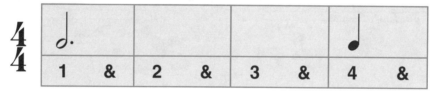

Dotted Quarter Note Rhythm

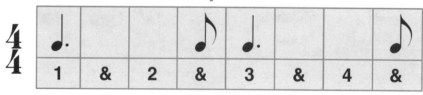

Dotted Eighth Note Rhythm

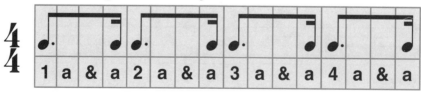

TAP the examples on a table top, hands separately, then together, counting aloud each time.

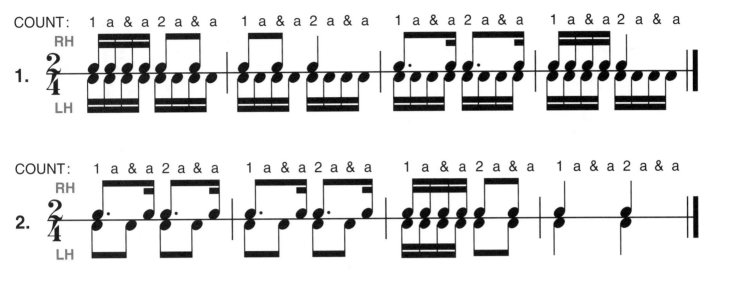

For each circle below, add the total number of beats that the notes would receive, assuming that a quarter note gets one count. Write the number on the line.

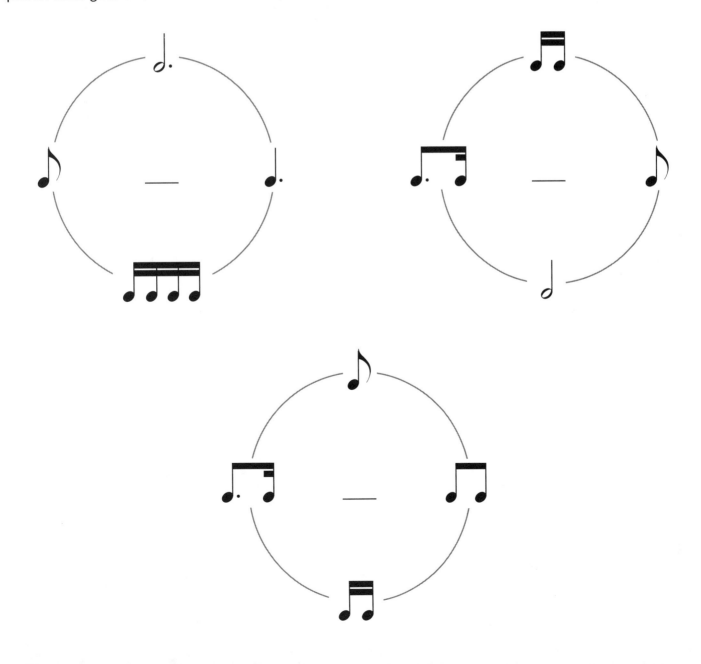

Quick Tambourine Dance

Martha Mier

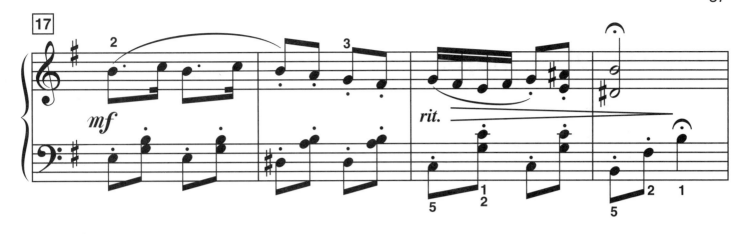

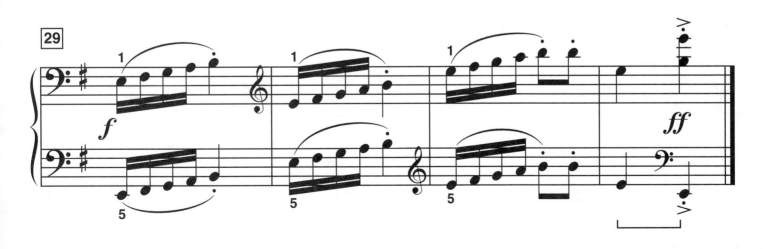

Use after page 39.

Unit 10

The Key of B♭ Major

The MAJOR SCALE is made of two tetrachords joined by a whole step.

The pattern of whole steps and half steps of a major scale is:

WHOLE STEP–WHOLE STEP–HALF STEP / WHOLE STEP / WHOLE STEP–WHOLE STEP–HALF STEP

Using the pattern of whole steps and half steps of the major scale, write the letter names of the B♭ MAJOR SCALE on the keys.

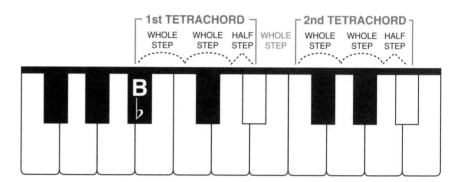

Using the pattern of whole steps and half steps of the major scale, write the notes of the B♭ MAJOR SCALE on the staff in both treble and bass clef. Use whole notes.

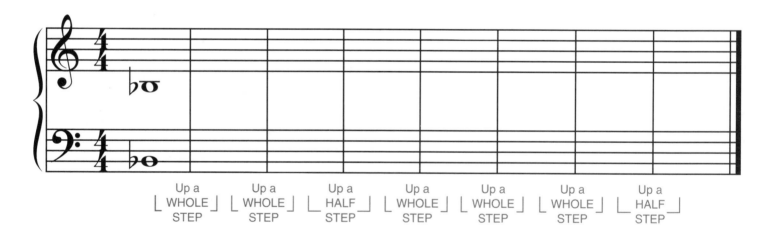

Play the B♭ major scale hands separately, then together.

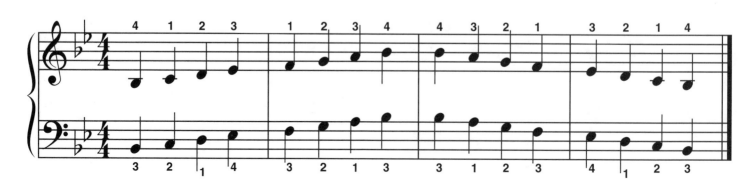

Primary Triads—Key of B♭ Major

The PRIMARY TRIADS are built on the 1st, 4th and 5th notes of the scale.
A seventh is often added to the **V** chord to create a seventh chord (**V⁷**).

Primary Triads in the Key of B♭ Major

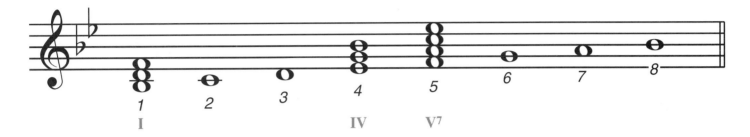

On the keyboards below, write the letter names for the notes of the primary triads
in the key of B♭ major.

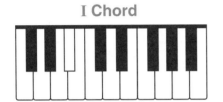
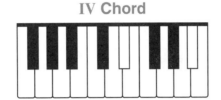
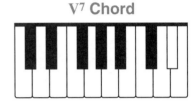

To make playing the **I**, **IV** and **V** (or **V⁷**) chords smoother moving from one to the other, the notes
may be rearranged. The same notes must be used, but they may be played in different octaves.

Practice the B♭ MAJOR CHORD PROGRESSION, hands separately, then together.
Say the chord names as you play.

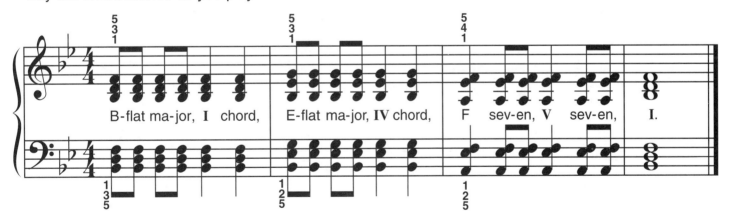

On the top line below the staff, write the Roman numeral name (**I**, **IV** or **V⁷**) of the chord
in the key of B♭ major.
On the bottom line, write the letter name (B♭, E♭ or F⁷) of the chord.

Roman Numeral: I ___ ___ ___ ___

Chord Name: B♭ ___ ___ ___ ___

Sweet Dreams of Home

Martha Mier

Slow waltz tempo

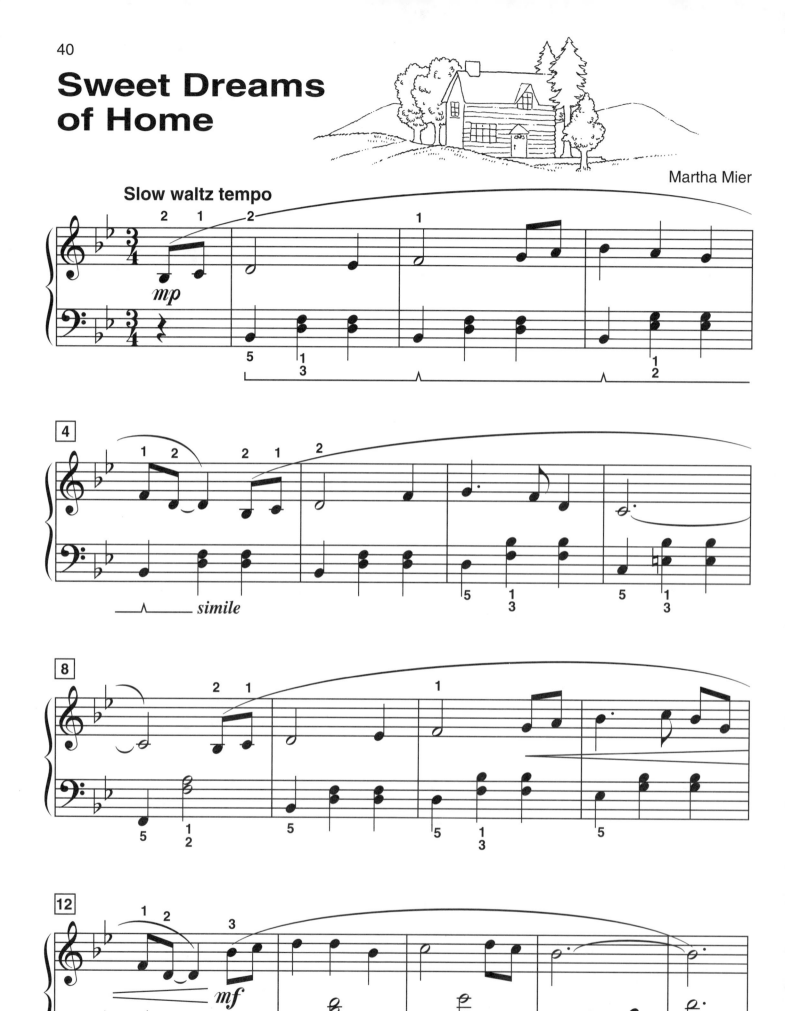

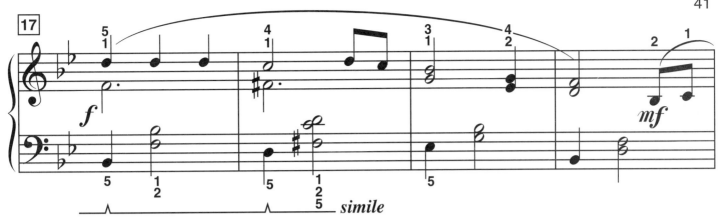

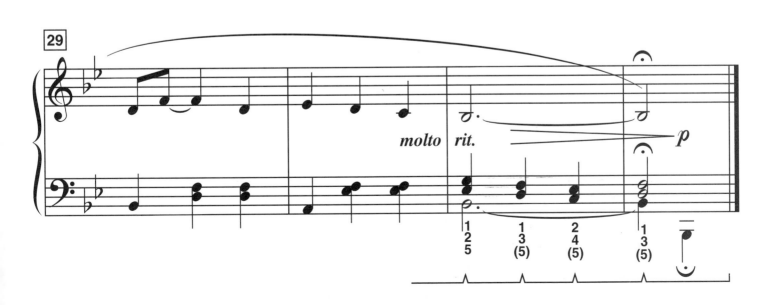

Use after page 43.

Unit 11

The Key of G Minor (Relative of B♭ Major)

Remember: Each major key has a RELATIVE MINOR key. It is called "relative" because it has the same key signature as the major key.

HOW TO FIND THE RELATIVE MINOR SCALE

The relative minor scale begins on the 6th tone of the major scale.

B♭ MAJOR SCALE

G MINOR SCALE

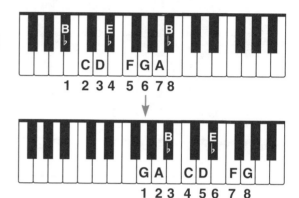

THE THREE KINDS OF MINOR SCALES

1. **NATURAL MINOR SCALE**

   This scale uses the tones of the relative major scale.

   On the keyboard, write the letters of the G NATURAL MINOR SCALE.

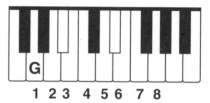

2. **HARMONIC MINOR SCALE**

   The 7th tone (F) is raised one half step, ascending and descending.

   On the keyboard, write the letters of the G HARMONIC MINOR SCALE.

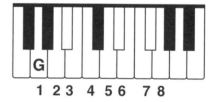

3. **MELODIC MINOR SCALE**

   In the ascending scale, the 6th (E♭) and 7th (F) tones are raised one half step. The descending scale is the same as the NATURAL MINOR.

   On the keyboards, write the letters of the G MELODIC MINOR SCALE, ascending and descending.

Ascending ⟶

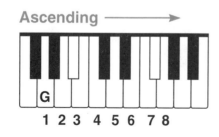

⟵ Descending

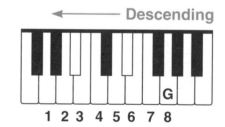

Using the fingering below, play the G natural, harmonic and melodic minor scales hands separately, then together, ascending and descending.

	Ascending	Descending
RH	1 2 3 1 2 3 4 5	5 4 3 2 1 3 2 1
LH	5 4 3 2 1 3 2 1	1 2 3 1 2 3 4 5

Primary Triads—Key of G Minor

The PRIMARY TRIADS are built on the 1st, 4th and 5th notes of the HARMONIC MINOR scale. Since the triads built on the 1st and 4th notes are minor triads, lower case Roman numerals are used (**i** and **iv**). The triad built on the 5th note is a major triad, so an upper case Roman numeral is used (**V**). A seventh is often added to the **V** chord to create a seventh chord (**V⁷**).

Primary Triads in the Key of G Minor

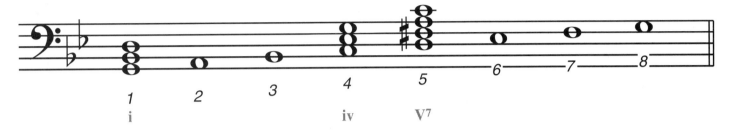

On the keyboards below, write the letter names for the notes of the primary triads in the key of G minor.

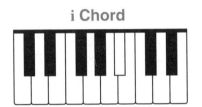
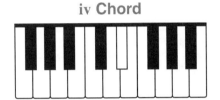
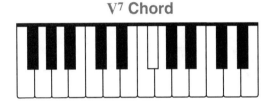

To make playing the **i**, **iv** and **V** (or **V⁷**) chords smoother moving from one to the other, the notes may be rearranged. The same notes must be used, but they may be played in different octaves.

Practice the following G MINOR CHORD PROGRESSION, hands separately, then together. Say the chord names as you play.

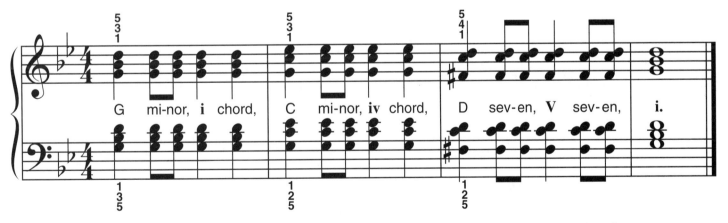

On the top line below the staff, write the Roman numeral name (**i**, **iv** or **V⁷**) of the chord in the key of G minor.
On the bottom line, write the letter name (Gm, Cm or D⁷) of the chord.

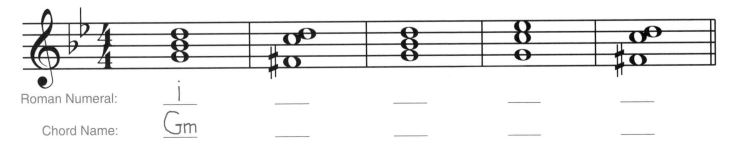

Roman Numeral: i   ___   ___   ___   ___

Chord Name: Gm   ___   ___   ___   ___

A Cloudy Day
in the Country

Martha Mier

Review Worksheet

Rhythm

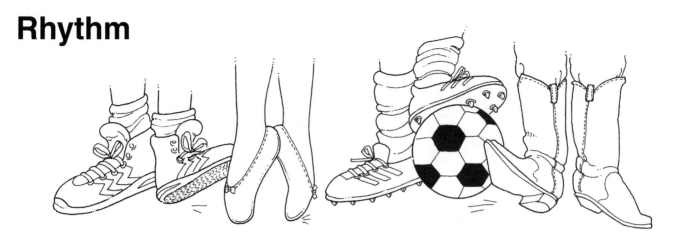

In each example below, cross out the box that contains a different number of counts from the others in the line. Assume that a quarter note gets one count.

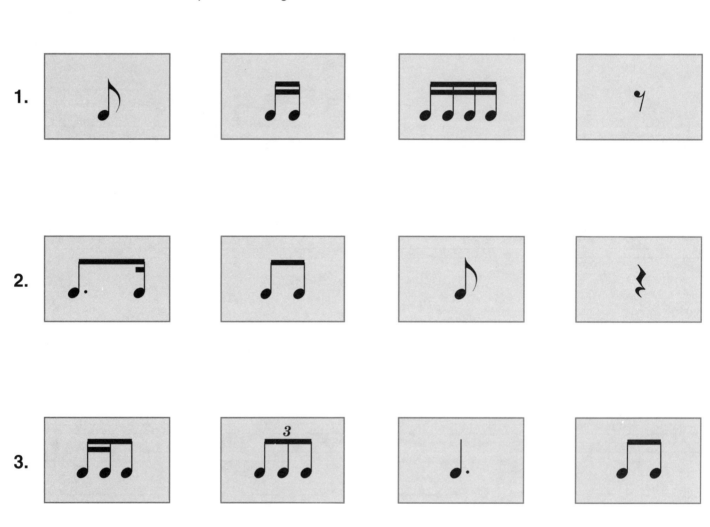

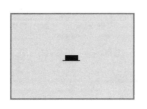

Review Worksheet

Primary Chords and Scales

Draw a line from each staff or keyboard to its matching label.

1.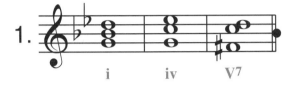

E MINOR
Primary Chords

2.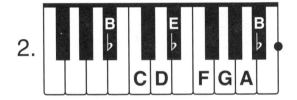

B♭ MAJOR
Scale

3.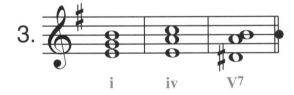

G MINOR
Primary Chords

4.

E HARMONIC MINOR
Scale

5.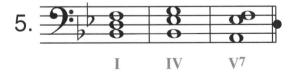

G HARMONIC MINOR
Scale

6.

B♭ MAJOR
Primary Chords

Crossword Puzzle

Complete the sentences below, then solve the crossword puzzle.

CLUES

1. Three-note chords (triads) have two inversions. Seventh chords have _____ inversions.

2. The tones of a triad consist of the root, third and _____ .

3. In a 1st inversion triad, the _____ is the lowest note.

4. ![bass clef triad] This is a _____ inversion triad.

5. In a 2nd inversion triad, the root is the _____ note.

6. ![treble clef triad] This is a _____ inversion triad.

7. ![bass clef triad] This is a _____ position triad.

8. In a root position triad, the root is the _____ note.

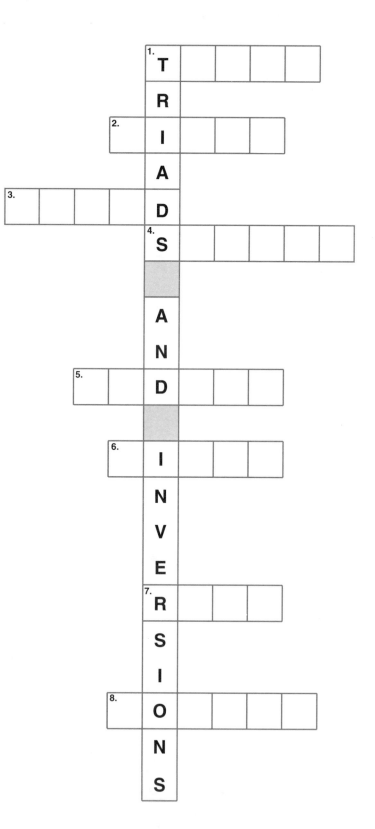

Use these word clues if necessary:

root, third, fifth, three, first, second, bottom, middle